# The Seasons I Called Life!!

Whispers of Feeling, Healing and Becoming!

Deepika

BookLeaf
Publishing

India | USA | UK

Made with ❤ on the BookLeaf Publishing Platform

www.bookleafpub.in

www.bookleafpub.com

# Dedication

This book is dedicated to every girl, every woman, who fights silent battles the world will never fully see — yet still chooses to rise.

To the ones who break stereotypes without seeking applause.
Who speak their truth even when their voice shakes.
Who fall, but never stay fallen.
Who carry storms in their minds, yet show up with grace.

To the women who take no disrespect — who swallow their pain, but never their power —
you are strength, you are softness, you are poetry.

This is for you.

You are absolute perfection — not because life is kind to you, but because you choose to stand again every single time it is not.

# Preface

Being an introvert and a writer is not as effortless as it may seem. Writing demands that you connect every word with your deepest emotions — but being an introvert means you grow up mastering the art of hiding them all beneath your skin. There is always a silent storm inside — thoughts that roar but never escape your lips.

By profession, I am an engineer — grounded in logic, systems, and precision. I love coding, playing with semicolons, syntax, and logic, there's an art even in those lines of code. But apart from programming languages, I've always been drawn to another kind of language — literature, where emotions find their voice. So, whenever emotions grow heavy and words begin to ache within me, I seek refuge in ink.

These unspoken layers hold stories of triumphs and failures that the world may never hear. Perhaps I never needed anyone to listen — or perhaps I was simply afraid of being judged, of hypocrisy more than loneliness.

But when the storm becomes too powerful to contain, it spills onto paper.

# Acknowledgements

To my father,
the one who never gave up on me, not even for a
moment.
Though you are no longer here with me, I know you
shine the brightest among the stars,
watching over me, guiding me, blessing me in silence.

Every step I take, every word I write, carries a part of
your strength and your faith in me.
This book is not just mine — it is yours, too.
Thank you for believing in me even before I believed in
myself.

# 1. The last time we met!!

The last time we met, I was trying to read your eyes,
and was wondering was it lying before or enunciating
the truth now.
I was continuously consoling my heart that the promise
of not
breaking the promises was meant to be broken somehow.

With that wide smile on the face, only I know how I had
answered
with that choked voice, when you asked "Are you fine".
I wanted to hold your hands for a little longer but
I knew they didn't want to be in mine.

I am still unanswered, was it that easy for you to forget
the laughs, the sobs and every emotions that we lived in
between.
Because, that day is still fresh in my head, when for the
first time,
your eyes had crossed mine and your shoulder made me
lean.

Your smile was not the same and neither were you,
and I could feel it in your voice that had never been so
low
So, as you wanted I didn't try to make you stay but
deep inside I never wanted you to go.

# 2. Let's call it love!!

Let's sit on the terrace,
with moon and stars above.
Let me curl my fingers around yours,
and just for a while, let's call it love.

Let's stroll down an empty street,
And while no one is noticing, let me dote on you
enough.
Let's talk about your favourites,
And just for a while, let's call it love.

Let's take a pause from rat, cat, or wolf races we are part
of,
And listen to each other's rants when days get tough.
Let me lean my head on your shoulder and breathe,
and just for a while, let's call it love.

Let's watch the night fade slowly,
as dawn paints skies above.

Let me hold your silence gently,
and just for a while, let's call it love.

# 3. All I need is you by my side!!

When nothing goes right even after endless tries,
and there is a complete roar thriving inside,
All I need is you by my side.

When what's wrong and what's right is hard to decide,
and life lacks a true guide,
All I need is you by my side.

When the heart feels heavy with oceans of emotions,
and the storm running in the head is not ready to
subside,
All I need is you by my side.

When the world turns against me
and life gets hit by high tide,
All I need is you by my side.

When fear grips tight and courage wants to hide,

and the path ahead feels too steep and wide,
All I need is you by my side.

# 4. Beside You, Always!!

I'll take you to the places you've never been,
No fear of being lost, nor left unseen.
We won't just rush from sight to sight,
rather, will sit in calm, where hearts feel light.
And there I'll hear, with patience and care,
The rants you've hidden, yet longed to share.

I'll make you taste the foods still untold,
New flavours waiting, fresh and bold.
But every feast, both first and last,
Will hold your favourites, unsurpassed.

I'll lead you to the dreams you've sought,
The daring things you once just thought.
And though you fear, don't be dismayed,
Beside you still, my hand will stay.

I'll show you wonders, strange and vast,
But guard your strength so joy will last.

And through it all, both near and far,
I'll pamper you with what you are.

# 5. Cherish the now!!

Hold their laughter close, like a sunshine in the rain,
A melody that soothes your deepest pain.
For time is fleeting, a thief in disguise,
A person, once gone, becomes memory in your eyes.

Speak the words that linger on your tongue,
The ones unsaid when your heart was young.
For silence, too, can bring regret,
A person, once gone, leaves a silence we fret.

keep their hands in yours often, and feel the hold,
Treasure the warmth before it turns cold.
Each hug, each touch, each shared delight,
A person, once gone, reminds us of lost light.

So cherish today, the now, the near,
Embrace with joy, dispel the fear.
For life's a moment, a fragile spree,
And a person, once gone, becomes memory, you see.

# 6. To be heard is to be held!!

In the quiet between words,
a world unfolds—
not of sound,
but of soul.

A voice finds its courage
only when it meets
an ear that does not hurry,
a heart that does not judge.

To be heard is to be held—
not by hands,
but by presence,
a cradle woven of attention,
where the fragile weight of truth rests unshaken.

The intimacy of being heard
outshines even touch,
for it says: you matter,
your silence, your tremor,

your tangled thoughts-
all have a place here.

And in that listening,
we are stitched back together,
not alone, but known.

# 7. I hope I never see you again!!

I hope I never see you again,
Not because I wish to part,
but to spare my heart that ache in vain.

Because I know it will never be as before,
When your smile made me insane and your touch
reached my heart's core.

Life's been pretty smooth since you left,
And my heart has already made peace with the fire you
had set.

It misses you sometimes, craves your presence as well,
But then I remind it of the days it spent in hell.

My heart and brain have not fought over you for a long
time.
Now, I don't fear losing you like earlier, when you were
already mine.

Your memories have always been good to me,
I visit them sometimes, not to meet you but to feel the
love no one can see.

I hope I never see you again,
Not because I wish to part,
but to spare my heart that ache in vain.

# 8. The quiet hands of love!!

Love will never ask you to change your name,
Nor dim your fire, nor shoulder the blame.
It won't whisper that you're asking too much,
Or weigh your worth in a shallow touch.


It won't make you shrink or feel you're less,
Or twist your truth in a silent press.
It won't be hunger masked as need,
Nor vanish quick when hearts may bleed.


Love is a freedom, not a chain,
A shelter strong in joy and pain.
It helps you rise, it helps you bloom,
It clears the path, it lifts the gloom.


Love waits, it listens, it takes its time,
It speaks not always, yet stays in rhyme.
It's not a game, not passing art-
It's the steady rhythm of a loyal heart.

When storms arrive, love does not flee,
It plants its roots, it dares to be.
Not selfish, not sudden, not just desire-
But quiet hands that never tire.

True love bears a noble weight,
Not just fate or random trait.
It takes the courage to stand, to stay,
To choose each other, come what may.

So know this truth, and hold it tight
Real love walks with patient light.
Not for show, or fleeting thrill-
But for the soul it longs to fill.

# 9. I still choose love!!

If loving you from the core of my heart was my idiocy, as
they say,
I am glad I was a fool, with a heart full of love who never
used emotions to play.

If giving you my heart and soul was my idiocy, as they
say,
I am glad I was a fool, who never knew you don't always
get back the same that you give away.

My mom had taught me the essence of love, I didn't
know what cheating and treachery mean.
Thanks to you for the new lesson on them— a new world
that I wish I had never seen.

It didn't make me stone-hearted, or harsh, or insensitive,
or anything like that,
In fact, it makes me proud that I loved selflessly, and
there's something I am really good at.

Believing that every fairy tale has a beautiful ending
might be a mistake,
But only a few have the courage to keep their everything
at stake.

I wasn't this fearless and valorous before,
I was, and I am, full of love — one who loves from the
heart's core.

# 10. Where are those days!!

Where are those days when love was pure, just like its
definition?
Where are those days when it could be expressed
through little gestures and actions?

Where are those days when promises were meant to be
kept anyhow,
And when "sticking through thick and thin" wasn't just
for a caption, but an unbreakable vow?

Where are those days when every moment mattered,
Not like now, where hearts chase the new and feel
flattered?

Where are those days when hearts looked for the best
within,
Instead of wandering among many and never settling in?

Where are those days when falling in love didn't need a
list of expectations,

a list that asks for everything except love and affection?

Where are those days when love could heal silent cries,
Not like an adventure to try someone new whenever
bored, with conversations full of lies.

Where are those days when two hearts would sit,
accept each other's flaws and make their relationship a
perfect fit?

Where are those days when love was not about lust,
But followed a magical journey built upon respect and
trust?

# 11. Grace in the storm!!

When waves of emotions crash your way,
ohh darling!!, what gives you the strength to stay?
To stand in storms where others fall,
you still choose to rise stronger through it all?

The world may try to dim your light,
Yet you keep shining, warm and bright.
You rise again, with fire untold,
What keeps your heart from turning cold?

When winds grow wild and skies turn gray,
How do you still find your way?
For every tear that leaves your eye,
You grow your wings and learn to fly.

Your hope's the spark that lights your pain,
You bloom again, through every rain.
So face your storms with fearless grace,
the world is yours, go claim your place.

# 12. Struggle for the existence and survival of the fittest!!

Days are passing by,
But wounds are not ready to heal.
Everything around me reminds me of you,
Ahhh! I just don't want to feel.

It feels like you are here only whenever I sink in,
Whispering strength when the darkness begins.
I long to share my joys and my fears,
And somehow feel you wipe away my tears.

And in those moments when the world feels too wide,
I feel your presence right by my side.
Not in body, but in every memory and glance,
Guiding me forward, giving me a chance.

Each day is a struggle to survive and life isn't fair since
you left,

Only a sentence from you keeps me going-
"Struggle for the existence and survival of the fittest".

# 13. You and They!!

Dear papa, why they can't be like you,
Yes 'YOU', who kept account of my elation without
giving a clue.
Yes YOU, who gave me hugs and kissed my cuts,
who pats my back and asks, not to get shut.

Papa, they stop me from being me,
blot out the world, I desire to see.
They have a series of do's and don'ts,
ohhh!the list really haunts.

I realised, I'm a girl when I moved out of your nest,
the place where you gave your girls your best.
Papa, they treat me like a girl,
the girl who is not allowed to make her own world.

But papa, your girl will not fall weak,
you only have made me strong not effete.
I promise, I won't be part of a crowd,
and someday, your girl will surely make you proud.

# 14. What if?

What if we had followed our hearts once more,
And painted dreams we left at the door?
What if we had danced in the rain,
Without fearing judgment, without the pain?

What if we had sung that song out loud,
Not caring who stared in the crowd?
What if we had chased that little spark,
That still flickers softly in the dark?

What if we had said the words we hid,
Those truths our trembling lips forbid?
For silence often leaves a deeper scar,
Than honesty ever could, by far.

What if we had shown our love on time,
Before the distance built its wall of crime?
What if we had held that hand once more,
Before it vanished beyond our shore?

What if we had sat with our elders awhile,
Listening to their tales with a patient smile?
What if we had taken that train one day,
To see them before time slipped away?
What if we had heard their laughter and sighs,
Before life whispered its quiet goodbyes?

What if we had listened to our inner voice,
Guiding us gently through each choice?
What if the future we dream tonight,
Turns into truth with morning light?

What if we had dared to live, not chase,
To slow our steps, to breathe, to embrace?
And what if—just once—we truly knew bliss,
**What if we would have got the answer of all our what
ifs?**

# 15. Since when?

Since when did we stop laughing our hearts out,
And start living in plans and future doubt?

Since when did we stop enjoying the now,
And get tangled in "what next" somehow?

Since when did we stop sharing life with friends,
And choose to hide the ache that never ends?

Since when did we start hurting others for our gain,
And forget that kindness eases pain?

Since when did we complain at every turn,
And stop thanking the stars for the light they burn?

Since when did disrespect become so cool,
And we stopped honouring the wise and old school?

Since when did we join the endless race,
Trading our smiles for a fleeting place?

Since when did we start hiding our emotions and call it
being strong,
As if being soft meant we didn't belong.

Since when did we stop folding hands to pray,
And question God through logic and clay?

Since when did we stop being who we are,
Just to belong, dimming our inner star?

# 16. Thank you, you!!

How did you always see the best in me,
When I had lost all faith in who I could be?

How did you listen to all my noise,
Yet still believe in my broken voice?

How did you smile when I shut the door,
When I wasn't myself anymore?

How were you patient, calm, and kind,
When I was chaos, out of my mind?

How did you stay when I pushed you away,
Stubborn and sharp in every way?

You made me laugh through the sleepless cries,
Found light for me when hope had died.

Even miles apart, you felt so near,
A voice I hold, so soft, so clear.

And how do you never cease to be,
The most amazing soul to me?

And honestly, I still wonder more,
If not that, what best friends are meant for.

# 17. If my scars could speak!!

If my scars could speak,
they would tell you indeed,
How difficult it gets even to breathe.

They'd tell you how it feels inside,
To be dying within, yet never confide.
To keep on going for those you love,
while breaking apart, yet no one knows of.

They would tell you, how difficult it gets to plaster the smile
on face when tears are on the verge,
and how difficult is to show up everyday
and pretend that still I have the urge.

They would tell you how it hurts to rise,
After sleepless night and heavy sighs-
How even small, day-to-day things,
can feel like battles no one sees.

If my scars could speak, they would softly tell
how mind becomes its own quiet hell,
How fear and anxiety never goes away
as there is a constant fear that no one is here to stay.

# 18. Your lessons, My strength!!

They wrote her rules in lines so neat,
What to wear, how to speak, how to greet.
A list of don'ts etched deep in dust,
As if her dreams were made to rust.

They praised the goddess carved in stone,
Yet shamed the girl who walked alone.
They sang of strength with folded hands,
But mocked the girl who takes a stand.

They called her wild, they called her wrong,
For choosing her path, for being strong.
The scars they gave, she wears with grace,
Each one a story time can't erase.

But her father's words, like morning dew,
Still whispers strength when the darkness grew:
"You're born to fly, not beg for air,
Let their gaze burn, but never care."

He taught her grace without the fear,
To walk through noise and still not hear.
"The world will change when you don't bend,
Your truth will be your loudest friend."

So when they called her wild, unwise,
She looked straight up at open skies.
For every chain they tried to form,
She built her wings — her calm, her storm.

# 19. Is being independent still my biggest turn on?

I still remember the day when, with millions of dreams,
I was moving to a city away from home.
Years later, here I am questioning myself,
is being independent still my biggest turn-on?

Things didn't turn out as crazy as I had imagined,
the inner me replied.
The gig nights and late-night parties are now replaced by
my bed,
perhaps the old me has somewhere died.

Now no one fights for the TV remote,
no one calls to say, "Come home early."
Sometimes, I just want to run away from this freedom,
and for a while... just live carefreely.

I miss the smell of morning tea,
and mom's voice echoing through the hall.
Those ghee dipped rotis and silly fights,

somehow, I miss them all.

A splendid house, a king-sized bed, all to myself,
Yet my heart still lives in the house, with that old
wooden shelf.
Where all of us slept on a single bed tight,
And talked till the morning replaced the night.

Now every memory feels like a feast untold,
memories full of warmth, more precious than gold.

# 20. I still wake up at 4!!

I still wake up at 4..!
The only thing that has changed is, then you were
memory clock
and now your memories are!!
Now, I trace your absence softly,
in those million shining stars.

I still go to our favourite place sometimes,
trying to find the same inner peace.
but then I realise it's never about the place
but the people who let our soul find ease.

I still linger over your old handwriting,
Each curve and word carrying your presence.
As you always said, people may leave,
But their energy stays, quietly, like a soft luminescence.

I still tell you all my stories, of the good days and the
bad,
Of my little wins, my failures, the moments happy and

sad.

Though you are not here with me, I know you are near,
Listening softly, and asking me not to fear.

# 21. There will be one morning when I'll  feel alive again!!

There will be one morning,
When my heart won't ache the way it does tonight.
When the weight I carry will quietly fade,
And I'll breathe without needing to fight.


When I'll smile, not because I should,
But because something inside me finally softens,
And the world will look a little more good.

When the mirror won't show the pain I hide,
When my eyes will hold light again,
And I'll stop searching for what died.

When the silence won't hurt anymore,
When I'll dance again to my own tune,
And not wait for footsteps at the door.

When I'll wake up to dreams, not memories.
When I'll walk ahead without trembling,
And trust the wind to carry my stories.

When I'll thank the night for what it taught,
For showing me that even broken things
Can bloom again—just not on the spot.

When I'll breathe, not just survive.
And that day, I'll whisper to myself—
You made it. You're truly alive.

# 22. Smile!!

Dear you,
The first thing they see, before you even speak,
Is that smile — tender, timeless, and unique.
A smile so stout-hearted, yet softly sweet,
That carries storms but never admits defeat.

It dances on your lips when life turns unfair,
When the nights are heavy with silent despair.
You wear it bravely through ache and through pain,
And somehow, the sun starts to shine again.

Your smile — it's the scent of earth after rain,
Petrichor soothing every heart's strain.
It bewitches the world, holds it still for a while,
Oh darling, there's magic within your smile.

Behind that smile lies a thousand unshed tears,
Dreams once whispered, lost in the years.
Yet you rise again, though the world may pry,
You smile — and even your sorrows sigh.

For that curve on your face is not mere delight,
It's battles fought quietly, night after night.
It's strength that speaks when words fall apart,
A silent hymn sung straight from your heart.

So never let it fade, never let it die,
Even when teardrops beg to ask why.
For that smile of yours, so fearless and true,
Holds the power to heal the universe — and you.

# 23. One last call!!

The phone rang soft, I heard his tone,
A voice so dear, yet tired and worn.
He spoke of days we used to share,
A silent wish to feel me there.

"Come home soon," he softly said,
A quiet ache, a heart that bled.
His breath was frail, yet laced with hope,
As if he knew, yet dared to cope.

"I'll see you soon," | promised light,
Unaware of fate's cruel might.
Destiny held me far, my hands were tied,
While he just longed for me beside.

His voice grew weak, yet still it stayed,
A whisper soft that wouldn't fade.
"Come home," he said, "just don't be late."
I never knew that this was fate.

The call went quiet, the line went dead,
His voice still echoed in my head.
And in the hush, I heard it all,
A father's love, in one last call.

# 24. This beautiful Life!!

Waking to the gift of a tender dawn,
Where golden light and hope are born.
Each breath reminds me, I belong,
To life's vast, ever-living song.

Living the dreams I used to chase,
Wrapped in love's eternal grace.
Among dear souls who make me whole,
Their warmth the shelter to my soul.

Walking through valleys, climbing the height,
Finding my calm in nature's light.
Each bloom, each breeze, each passing hue,
A silent blessing the heavens drew.

Smiling through days both soft and tough,
Knowing this life is more than enough.
Each breath, each beat, a tender sigh-
A hymn of love to this beautiful life.

# 25. It's 3 a.m. again!!

It's 3 a.m., the world's asleep,
and here I am, with thoughts too deep.
My dearest friends — my pen and diary —
sit beside me, calm yet fiery.

But tonight, something feels untrue,
for both refused to write of you.
My pen fell silent, cold and still,
my diary denied my will.

They said their friends have roamed afar —
through mountain mist and fields of stars.
They've traced the valleys, sketched the sea,
and inked the hues of poetry.

While here I sit, both night and noon,
writing your name beneath the moon.
They say their friends meet souls each day,
but mine knows only you — always.

They laughed and said, "You write, but not to feel —
your ink has lost its old appeal."
And maybe they were right, I guess —
I built my cage from tenderness.

Tonight, they asked me to decide —
to choose my peace or stay confined.
And strangely, without guilt or pain,
I chose my pen — and broke your chain.